Pri

and

Humility

Pride and Humility

*A Discourse, Setting Forth the Characteristics
of the Proud and the Humble*

also

An Alarm to the Proud

By John M. Brenneman

SERMON ON THE MOUNT
PUBLISHING

Manchester, MI

ISBN 978-1-68001-025-1

For additional titles and other material by the same author, contact:

Sermon on the Mount Publishing
P.O. Box 246
Manchester, MI 48158
(734) 428-0488
the-witness@sbcglobal.net
www.kingdomreading.com

Our Mission
To obey the commands of Christ and to teach men to do so.

Acknowledgements

Thanks to all those who have made this project possible, including Vincent, Barbara, Faith, and Grace Ste. Marie for their help in ensuring the accuracy of the text; Joe Springer and the staff of the Mennonite Historical Library at Goshen College, for their ever-ready help in locating needed resources and, particularly, Joe's identification of Brenneman's allusion to a poem on the beard; Edsel Burdge, for his invaluable input on the project, particularly aiding in the identification of some of Brenneman's obscure quotations; Aaron Burkholder for translating and Leonard Gross for reviewing the translation of Brenneman's German poem; Mike Atnip and Chester Weaver for their comments on the Historical Introduction; Jennifer Burdge, for copyediting; and Mike Atnip, for the cover design and layout help. May the Lord give you all His grace.

Most of all, thanks and praise to Jesus Christ, the Lord of the humble.

Pride and Humilty:

A

DISCOURSE,

Setting forth the Characteristics of the Proud and
the Humble.

By John M. Brenneman.

Elkhart, Indiana:

JOHN F. FUNK.

1867.

Title page of the first edition of *Pride and Humility*.

Historical Introduction

For centuries, Anabaptist/Mennonites had suffered in Europe. Persecuted in varying degrees by both Catholic and Protestant governments, Anabaptists believed that nonresistant suffering was a defining mark of true Christianity.

Upon arriving in North America, lured by promises of religious toleration, military exemption, and economic prosperity, continued emphasis on suffering made less and less sense. How could suffering continue to be the defining mark of true Christianity, when sincere Christians were prosperous and no longer persecuted by the government? More than one answer was suggested, but a change of emphasis was the result of this conceptual tension. Mennonites emphasized another early Anabaptist theme, humility, as the defining essence of true Christianity.

Beginning in the colonial period, Mennonites began to articulate what has been called a "humility theology." Spiritual conversion must change someone from pride to humility, they said. Humility, while it is an inner attitude, is easily discerned by one's outward behavior. One's clothing, possessions, wealth, and attitudes – his obedience (or lack thereof) to God and the church – betrayed whether pride or humility was ascendant in his heart. Pride and violence became the defining characteristics of the world; humility and nonresistance, the defining characteristics of the Christian.

By the time of John M. Brenneman (1816-1895), this humility theology was well-entrenched in Mennonite and Amish thinking. In 1866, Brenneman's three-part essay on "Pride and Humility" was published in the June, July, and August issues of the Mennonite paper *Herald of Truth*. The articulate and compelling presentation received an enthusiastic response, and in 1867 an enlarged edition was published as a booklet.

"This booklet did not influence his [Brenneman's] generation's understanding of humility," one historian has written; "in fact Brenneman said nothing new on the topic. What he did was to say well and fully what his peers said fumblingly and partially."[1]

---

1   Joseph C. Liechty, "Humility: The Foundation of the Mennonite Religious Outlook in the 1860s," *Mennonite Quarterly Review* 54(1) (January 1980): p. 13.

One appreciative response published by the *Herald of Truth* said that

> Christ was a pattern of humility and his whole life was an exposition of the truth which he professed and taught. And as humility was one of the distinguishing characteristics in the life of our Saviour, so must it also be in the lives of his followers. It is not enough that they profess themselves to be humble; they must declare, also, in their actions and with their apparel, that they are humble. They must let the light of humility shine before men, that they may see it and glorify our Father which is in heaven.[2]

The letter-writer concluded that "Humility is the best evidence of true piety, and the most humble man or woman is the most eminent Christian, and such shall be greatest in the kingdom of heaven. We may measure the advancement of piety in our souls by the increase of humility."[3]

Pride and Humility was released as a booklet in both English and German in 1867 at the retail price of eight cents. *Herald of Truth* said that "A copy should be in every household."[4] By March 1868, the English edition was sold out, and a reprint was released in June, at the postpaid retail price of ten cents each. It continued to be well-received by Mennonites; one Virginia bishop wrote to the *Herald*:

> Enclosed I send you 75 cents for which you will please send me another dozen of Pride and Humility. I have just read through one of these pamphlets, and am so well pleased with it that I feel it my duty to distribute them among the people. To those that will not buy I give them as a present.
>
> I think the brethren and sisters every where ought to buy them, not only for the use of their own families but also to distribute among others.[5]

---

2   Samuel Godshalk, "Letter from Bucks Co., Pa.," *Herald of Truth* 3(10) (October 1866):82.

3   *Ibid.*

4   "Pride and Humility," *Herald of Truth* 4(6) (June 1867):88.

5   Jacob Hildebrand, "Pride and Humility," *Herald of Truth* 8(6) (June 1871):91.

In 1873, a third edition was released. This edition included a new essay, "Alarm to the Proud," as well as some new poems and several quotations from non-Mennonite works against ostentatious dress. The *Herald* said that it "is a work which cannot be too carefully nor too frequently read in the present extravagant age."[6]

Brenneman's work became a classic, reprinted several times in both English and German in the decades following his death. The present edition presents the full text of the third (1873) edition, including additional material such as "Alarm to the Proud." All illustrations, Scripture reference footnotes, and subheadings are the publisher's additions. Other unsigned footnotes are Brenneman's. Some slight modifications in punctuation use have been made.

This work is not reprinted simply to give a theology of humility, or to serve as a specimen of someone else's humility theology. It is rather reprinted to exhort readers to humility – the reason Brenneman wrote the book in the first place. As Brenneman said, "Examine yourself seriously and critically by the mirror here placed before you, and consider well what is your character and to which class you belong, whether to the proud or the humble. . . If you find yourself still in the way of the proud, turn, oh! turn, and have compassion on yourself, O man!"

Andrew V. Ste. Marie
February 5, 2018

---

6   "Pride and Humility," *Herald of Truth* 10(5) (May 1873):88.

Original Preface

The following essay on PRIDE AND HUMILITY appeared some
time ago in the HERALD OF TRUTH, and is now published in
pamphlet form with additions and improvements, at the request
of some of the brethren who have thought it proper and needful
to republish the same for distribution, as a warning and a call to
the proud, and an admonition and encouragement to all Christian
believers, especially Mennonites, to remind them of their duties
toward themselves and their children. May the God of grace
(without whose help[1] all our efforts are vain) grant his blessing
on this humble work, which was written from good motives,
and may it be a powerful and effectual voice of warning to many
hearts, to convict them and move them to reflect, in this precious
day of grace, on their soul's eternal salvation and peace. Yea,
God grant that it may be a refreshment and a blessing to many a
lukewarm and weary heart, and that it may redound to his honor
alone, is the ardent prayer of the humble writer. Amen.

J.M.B.

---

1   The 1867 and 1868 editions include "and blessing."—*Ed.*

Pride and Humility

"God resisteth the proud, and giveth grace to the humble."

1 Pet. 5:5

The apostle Peter begins this chapter with an exhortation to the elders or teachers, as to the manner in which they should care for the flock of Christ, which was committed to their charge. "Feed the flock of God which is among you," he says, "taking the oversight thereof, not by constraint, but willingly; not for filthy lucre, but of a ready mind: neither as being lords over God's heritage, but being ensamples to the flock. And when the chief Shepherd shall appear, ye shall receive a crown of glory that fadeth not away," and which is of many thousand times greater value, than the filthy gains of this world can ever be worth.

He then proceeds to admonish the younger to be subject to the elder; which is at all times proper and well worthy still to be observed by our younger brethren and sisters in this our day. And finally, he exhorts all believers in general, saying, "Yea, all of you be subject one to another, and be clothed with humility," and then adds as a reason for so doing that "God resisteth the proud, and giveth grace to the humble." With these words he gave them clearly to understand that, as long as they seek to exalt themselves one over another and do not yield themselves in subjection one to another, it is clear evidence that they are not yet humble, but proud and filled with a spirit of exaltation.

The text treats of two entirely distinct classes of persons, which are as unlike and as opposed to each other as light is to darkness, or day to night. The proud constitute one class; the humble, the other. The one class God resists; to the other he gives grace.

Dear readers, it is through a sense of duty and love to my fellow-men, that I feel inwardly pressed to set forth, with the help of the Lord, in as clear a light as possible, for the edification of pilgrim travelers to a long eternity the exceeding great difference between these two classes of persons. That all may prove to which class they belong, may God direct and control my thoughts and mind as is pleasing to him, that it may redound to his honor and to the edification of my readers. Amen.

"God resisteth the proud." The pride of men is very displeasing to God, and is reckoned among the abominations of the wicked, Rom. 1:30; 2 Tim. 3:2. It is directly the opposite to humility, and is placed in direct contrast with it in the text, as also in other passages: as, "A man's pride shall bring him low: but honor shall uphold the humble in spirit," Prov. 29:23. "The eyes of the lofty shall be humbled," Isa. 5:15.

In contrast with humility, the terms, "lofty," "lifted up," "haughty," "high-minded" and "arrogant," are also used, which, in this connection express very nearly the same idea as that implied in the word proud; as in the following passages: "Behold every one that is proud, and abase him," Job 40:11. "When his heart was lifted up, and his mind hardened in pride, he was deposed from his kingly throne, and they took his glory from him. And thou, his son, O Belshazzar, hast not humbled thine heart, though thou knewest all this," Dan. 5:20-22. "Those that walk in pride he is able to abase," Dan. 4:37. "When pride cometh, then cometh shame; but with the lowly is wisdom," Prov. 11:2.

I believe that he who is proud, is also high-minded and haughty, as may be clearly seen from passages like these: "We have heard the pride of Moab (he is exceedingly proud), his loftiness, and his arrogancy, and his pride, and the haughtiness of his heart," Jer. 48:29. "I will cause the arrogancy of the proud to cease, and will lay low the haughtiness of the terrible," Isa. 13:11. "The beginning of pride is when one departeth from God, and his heart is turned away from his Maker. For pride is the beginning of sin, and he that hath it shall pour out abomination: and therefore the Lord brought upon them strange calamities, and overthrew them utterly. The Lord hath cast down the thrones of proud princes, and set up the meek in their stead. The Lord hath plucked up the roots of the proud nations, and planted the lowly in their place," Ecclesiasticus 10:12-15.[1]

A proud man has a puffed up and conceited mind, commonly esteeming himself very highly, and regarding others with con-

---

[1]   Ecclesiasticus or Wisdom of Solomon is a book in the Old Testament Apocrypha.—*Ed.*

tempt, or as unworthy of notice, and imagines that every one should bend in submission to him, whilst he in his exaltation frequently looks down on them with scorn, contempt and derision. He is conceited and high-minded, and thinks that he is better and smarter than other people, and does not like to receive reproof or advice. In short, he is usually a man of haughty, overbearing, imperious, vain-glorious, ambitious, self-exalted and high-minded disposition, and desires to be in the society of the great of the world, to be equal to them, and, if possible, to be the first among them. He loves to talk of himself, of his possessions, of his deeds, and abilities, and likes to be praised and held in high esteem by the people.

The word "proud" is applied to various kindred qualities of character. It is used as descriptive of the man "that," as Buechner[2] says, "especially manifests, by his manner of deportment, a feeling of superiority over others, or of importance which he assumes to himself, and of honor which, in his opinion, is due to him, being especially desirous also, to enjoy the honors of an exalted station and wealth, and giving evidence of the same by a special show of splendor and magnificence. He is also vain and ostentatious."

And again, Buechner says of this class, "They make an ill use of the respects bestowed on them, wish to be more highly esteemed than others, are conceited, use much ceremony in what they do, treat others with disdain, despise and even oppress them." Again he says, "The proud man is sunk in self-love, elates himself, elevates himself above others, forgets God and is unwilling to render to him due obedience for his love, imagines that his way of doing things only is right, and tries to carry out all his plans with a haughty ambition."[3] Pride, like many other evil things, proceeds from within, out of the heart, and defiles the man, Mark 7:22.

Its origin is of Satan, who was the first that fell thereby. And because he was envious and hostile towards man, who was created noble and glorious, he came haughtily to our mother Eve and by cunning and deceit persuaded her, that they would "not surely

---

2   M. Gottfried Büchner (1701-1780) was a German Lutheran theologian.
3   M. Gottfried Büchner, *Biblische Real- und Verbal-Hand-Concordanz oder Exegetisch-homiletisches Lexikon*, 1859, C. U. Schwetschke und Sohn.

die"[4] by eating the forbidden fruit. And by his haughty and deceit-ful spirit he planted in her heart the seeds of pride; for by persuad-ing her that she and Adam, by eating of the fruit would become wise like God, he excited in her a desire to become wise, and "when the woman saw that the tree was good for food, and that it was pleasant to the eyes, and a tree to be desired to make one wise, she took of the fruit thereof, and did eat, and gave also unto her husband with her; and he did eat. And the eyes of them both were opened, and they knew that they were naked."[5] Hence, from the sin of Pride arose the necessity of wearing clothes. Here they fell through pride; for if they had remained steadfast in humility, they would not have fallen.

Man fell by pride

Thus by pride man fell, and it is only through humbleness of heart that he can be restored. We can here clearly see whence the origin of the great evil, pride, is. I think it may justly be called the Serpent's seed, which was planted in our first parents, and from them all their posterity became infected and poisoned with the same. Hence, "pride was the first sin, and will be the last to be overcome," as has been said. O detestable vice, the source of so great evil, from which none but the Lamb of God can deliver us! Pride exists, by nature, in man, in a greater or less degree, as long as he is not regenerated, and has not yet been changed from his old nature to a state of humility. Pride in a man's heart cannot remain concealed, but, like the fruit of a tree, will crop out, and manifest itself in look and gestures. "Him that hath a high look and a proud heart will not I suffer," Ps. 101:5. "A high look and a proud heart is sin," Prov. 21:4. A man's words oftentimes proclaim his pride. "With their mouth they speak proudly," Ps. 17:10. In short, it manifests itself and may be known by a man's actions, deeds, and manner of deportment; as, for instance, in the case of the builders of the tower of Babel. "Let us build us a city," they said, "and a tower whose top may reach unto heaven; and let us make us a name."[6] This was an exceedingly haughty and presumptuous

4   Genesis 3:4.
5   Genesis 3:6-7.
6   Genesis 11:4.

Pride likes to be seen and to make great display,
in order to make itself "a name."

undertaking. But pride is of such a nature that it cannot and
will not be hid: it likes to be seen and to make great display, in
order to make itself "a name." It is also far too prevalent in our
days and is clearly visible in the needless splendor, costliness,
and magnitude of houses, barns, &c., which are sometimes
highly ornamented, and painted in a variety of colors, merely
to make a magnificent show. It is frequently also to be seen in
the manner in which houses are adorned and furnished within,
being, like palaces, splendidly ornamented and fitted up with
all kinds of new-fashioned, ornamental, and costly furniture,
floors overspread with brilliant and showy carpeting, windows
decorated with fine drapery, and walls adorned with pictures.
Even among non-resistant professors of Christianity, may
be seen some very unsuitable ornaments such as portraits of
military heroes and officers armed with the instruments of
death! The tables also are often strewed over with likenesses
of mortal and deceased persons, which parents, children, and
friends had taken, although it is strictly forbidden. Ex. 20:4,
Deut. 4:16, and 5:8. These lifeless pictures must then also
be frequently looked at and exhibited to others. This, I fear,

is "lust of the eyes," and pride of life. O, that we were so intent also on regaining the lost and noble image of God, and willing to labor that Christ may be formed in us! I believe sincerely that, if this image of God be effectually and truly formed within us, we shall feel but little concerned about these vain and perishable likenesses. Again, an evidence of pride is also seen in the costliness and extravagant manner of serving tables, each one desiring to equal or, if possible, to surpass the other in making great preparations and bestowing needless attentions and acts of politeness in imitation of the higher and fashionable classes of the world. Evidences of pride may also be seen in the costly and splendidly ornamented coaches and carriages, and in many other ways that cannot be here enumerated.

Pride manifested

But especially does pride, when it exists in the heart, manifest itself very plainly in the manner of dress and in the costly array with which poor dying mortals strive, frequently beyond their means, to decorate themselves, in order to gain the respect and esteem of a proud and wicked world. Indeed, many dress in the very height of fashion, adorning themselves in the highest style of the world, and withal consider themselves good Christians. If such things can be pleasing to God, I must confess, that I have yet but little knowledge of the word of God and of true Christianity. Many, with all their pomp and decorations, still justify themselves by saying, it does not matter so much about the externals, if only the heart is right. It is very true indeed that a good heart is the essential qualification in the true Christian character; but a good heart, beyond doubt, is also humble, and consequently cannot exhibit any pride; for "a good man, out of the good treasure of the heart, bringeth forth good things."[7] I know there are persons who say that the religion of the Mennonites consists entirely in their manner of dress, and that, in their estimation, the style of dress decides the whole matter. But if this were true, then the state of the Mennonites would indeed be sad to contemplate; for if they had no other Christianity than what they carry in their dress,

---

7   Matthew 12:35a.

A plainly-dressed Mennonite couple is contrasted with a fashionable couple of the same time frame (mid-1800s).

they would not have any at all. God forbid that a true Mennonite should believe that Christianity consists merely in simplicity of dress.

A genuine and true Mennonite assuredly believes that true Christianity is to be found only in the humble and regenerate heart, and that out of such a heart can proceed or be manifested no fruits of pride: but that it will much rather feel an aversion to, and abhor, all needless ornament and extravagance in dress. It is sadly true, however, that in our day there are some also who call themselves Mennonites, but indulge in the extravagancies of dress and fashion, considering themselves good Christians withal and maintaining that it can make no difference what kind of dress one wears. But I think the name Mennonite is very unsuitable for such persons, as long as their manner of life is so directly contrary to the teachings of Menno. I am well aware that merely the name Mennonite will not profit us in the least, if we are not true Christians. Therefore, ye proud Mennonites (the humble are not meant), hear what Menno thinks of extravagance in dress. In his treatise on the faith of the woman whose sins Christ forgave, he says: "When *she* believed, her proud, worldly, haughty heart became humble, meek, and contrite. But *they* (pretended Christians) say they believe, though they indulge, without measure or restraint, in cursed pride, in foolish extravagance and superfluity of silks, velvets, costly raiment, gold rings, and chains, belts, pins, and buttons of silver, finely embroidered and ornamented shirts, cravats, collars, hoods, veils, aprons, velvet slippers, and many other like follies, not considering that the highly enlightened apostles Paul and Peter have in clearly expressed language forbidden all Christian women thus to adorn their outward person; and consequently it is much more unbecoming in men, who are the examples to, and the head of the woman, to indulge in such extravagances."[8]

And of the kingdom of Christ he says, page 96, "This is not a kingdom in which a display is made of gold, silver, pearls, silk, velvet, and costly finery, as is done by the proud, wicked world... but it is the kingdom of all humility, in which, (I say) not the outward adorning of the body, but the inward adorning of the spirit is sought and desired with great power, zeal and diligence, with a broken heart and a contrite spirit."[9]

And again he says, "true believers walk honorably and modestly, avoid all manner of pride and superfluity, and make

---

8   These quotations from Menno Simons are Brenneman's own translations, made from the 1835 Lancaster edition of the *Fundamentbuch*. Menno Simons, *True Christian Faith*, c. 1541; translated from Menno Simons, *Ein Fundament und Klare Anweisung*, 1835, Johann Bär, p. 364. cf. contemporary English translations in: *The Complete Works of Menno Simons*, First Part, 1871, John F. Funk and Brother (reprinted 1983, Pathway Publishers), p. 144; also, J. C. Wenger, ed., *The Complete Writings of Menno Simons*, 1956, Herald Press, p. 377.

9   This quotation, added in the third (1873) edition of *Pride and Humility*, is referenced by Brenneman to John F. Funk's English edition of Menno's writings. The first sentence is identical to Funk's version, but Brenneman appears to have translated the second sentence himself. Menno Simons, *Foundation of Christian Doctrine*, 1539-40, 1558; translated from Menno Simons, *Ein Fundament und Klare Anweisung*, 1835, Johann Bär, p. 234; *The Complete Works of Menno Simons*, First Part, 1871, John F. Funk and Brother (reprinted 1983, Pathway Publishers), p. 96. cf. J. C. Wenger, ed., *The Complete Writings of Menno Simons*, 1956, Herald Press, p. 217.

or desire no other clothes than those necessary for daily comfort and convenience."[10] And further he says, "I, therefore, entreat you all, ye women, through the mercy of the Lord, that you take this poor, penitent sinner as an example, imitate her faith, humble yourselves before the Lord, renounce all your avarice, pride, uncleanness, and wickedness, and do not adorn yourselves with gold, silver, pearls, braided hair, or costly array; but use such apparel as becomes those professing godliness, and is needful in your labors."[11]

The above, I think, shows plainly enough what Menno Simons' views were in regard to ornament in dressing. But a greater than Menno is here. God himself testifies abundantly against it in his word, which is all the testimony we need; although there are those who say, the Mennonites have no ground in Scripture for their simple mode of dress. Such persons must have but very superficial knowledge of the Scriptures, or they willingly ignore these things. Whether simplicity of dress is but a human conceit; that is, whether it makes very little difference, how we dress ourselves, let the impartial reader judge, after reading what is said below. God himself made unto Adam and Eve coats, not of silk or costly linen, but of skins. This, it seems to me, was quite a simple form of dress, intended not for ornament, but simply as a covering to their nakedness. That the outward adorning of the person is exceedingly displeasing to the Lord may be plainly seen from Ex. 33:4-6, "Say unto the children of Israel, Ye are a stiff-necked people: I will come up into the midst of thee in a moment and consume thee: therefore now put off thy orna-

---

10   Menno Simons, *True Christian Faith*, c. 1541; translated from Menno Simons, *Ein Fundament und Klare Anweisung*, 1835, Johann Bär, p. 372. cf. contemporary English translations in: *The Complete Works of Menno Simons*, First Part, 1871, John F. Funk and Brother (reprinted 1983, Pathway Publishers), p. 147; also, J. C. Wenger, ed., *The Complete Writings of Menno Simons*, 1956, Herald Press, p. 381.

11   Menno Simons, *True Christian Faith*, c. 1541; translated from Menno Simons, *Ein Fundament und Klare Anweisung*, 1835, Johann Bär, p. 375. cf. contemporary English translations in: *The Complete Works of Menno Simons*, First Part, 1871, John F. Funk and Brother (reprinted 1983, Pathway Publishers), p. 148; also, J. C. Wenger, ed., *The Complete Writings of Menno Simons*, 1956, Herald Press, p. 383.

Which dress better
represents pride and
which better represents
humility?

ments from thee, that I may know what to do unto thee. And
the children of Israel stripped themselves of their ornaments
by the mount Horeb." And Deut. 22:5, "The woman shall not
wear that which pertaineth unto a man, neither shall a man put
on a woman's garment: for all that do so are abomination unto
the Lord thy God." And Isa. 3:16-24, "Moreover the Lord saith,
Because the daughters of Zion are haughty, that is proud, and walk
with stretched forth necks and wanton eyes, walking and mincing
as they go, and making a tinkling with their feet: Therefore the
Lord will smite with a scab the crown of the head of the daughters
of Zion. In that day the Lord will take away the bravery of their
tinkling ornaments about their feet, and their cauls [or, hairnets,
which are now so prevalent], and their round tires like the moon,
The chains, and the bracelets, and the mufflers, The bonnets, and
the ornaments of the legs, and the headbands, and the tablets, and
the ear-rings, The rings, and nose jewels, The changeable suits of
apparel, and the mantles, and the wimples, and the crisping pins,
The glasses, and the fine linen, and the hoods, and the vails. And

it shall come to pass, that instead of sweet smell there shall be stink; and instead of a girdle a rent; and instead of well set hair baldness; and instead of a stomacher a girding of sackcloth; and burning instead of beauty."

Explanation is not necessary here. The Lord threatens, in very plain language, to take from the daughters of Zion (the church of God is sometimes called Zion) their outward ornaments. And in Ezek. 23 he threatened to bring against the rebellious city of Jerusalem a people, before whom he would set judgment, that they might judge her, and he says (ver. 26), "They shall also strip thee out of thy clothes, and take away thy fair jewels." And "it shall come to pass in the day of the Lord's sacrifice, that I will punish the princes, and the king's children, and all such as are clothed with strange apparel," Zeph. 1:8. John the Baptist "had his raiment of camel's hair, and a leathern girdle about his loins."[12] This, it seems to me, must have been a very plain and simple garment. Jesus, speaking of John, said, "What went ye out for to see? A man clothed in soft raiment? Behold, they which are gorgeously appareled, and live delicately, are in kings' courts," Luke 7:25. To be gorgeously appareled and to live delicately seem to belong together. Do the followers of Jesus live delicately? Do they love to be in kings' courts? Are they not mostly of the poorer and humble classes of people? Yet there may sometimes be rich persons among them; but to such Paul's admonition, "Charge them that are rich in this world, that they be not high-minded" (1 Tim. 6:17), will be highly necessary.

Jesus says, "There was a certain rich man, which was clothed in purple and fine linen and fared sumptuously every day."[13] And further he says, "In hell he lifted up his eyes, being in torment."[14] Jesus does not say that he was otherwise an open, turbulent sinner. It seems as though Jesus had in view the voluptuous garments and the sumptuous fare, as being the main causes of his damnation. James warned the brethren that they should not have respect to a rich man in gay clothing in preference to a poor man in vile raiment, Jas. 2:2, 3. The scribes were mostly high-minded persons.

---

12   Matthew 3:4.
13   Luke 16:19.
14   Luke 16:23a.

Jesus, therefore, censured them, saying, "Beware of the scribes, which desire to walk in long robes, and love greetings in the markets, and the highest seats in the synagogues, and the chief rooms at feasts," Luke 20:46. Here it seems to me, Jesus considered the desire to "walk in long robes" equally as much an indication of pride as the desire to hold the "highest seats" and "chief rooms."

Peter expressly forbids women to adorn their outward person with plaiting of the hair, and the wearing of gold, or the putting on of apparel; "but," says he, "let it be the hidden man of the heart, in that which is not corruptible, even the ornament of a meek and quiet spirit, which is in the sight of God of great price."[15] "For after this manner, in the olden time, the holy women also who trusted in God, adorned themselves,"[16] which still, at the present time, would be very becoming to them and acceptable to God.

This inward adorning may consist, in part, of that which the apostle Paul (Col. 3:12-14) enjoins, saying, "Put on, as the elect of God, holy and beloved, bowels of mercies, kindness, humbleness of mind, meekness, long-suffering; and above all these things put on charity, which is the bond of perfectness." "The king's daughter (bride or wife) is all glorious within: her clothing is of wrought gold," Ps. 45:13.

Paul says, "I will that women adorn themselves in modest apparel, with shamefacedness and sobriety; not with braided hair, or gold, or pearls, or costly array; but (which becometh women professing godliness) with good works," 1 Tim. 2:9, 10. How could anything be more clearly forbidden, than the putting on of costly ostentatious apparel, is here forbidden? Therefore, by commanding women to adorn themselves with modest apparel, the apostle gives them clearly to understand that they should not be immodest, extravagant or ostentatious, but that due moderation in the putting on of apparel, as also in all other things, should be observed with shamefacedness and sobriety. He gives us clearly to understand also that, in those times, as is the case in our day, extravagance in dress and personal adornment were prevalent; and he further teaches, that women should adorn themselves as becomes those professing godliness (Christianity) with good works.

---

15   1 Peter 3:4.
16   1 Peter 3:5.

From this we may infer that there prevailed a style of apparel that was unbecoming for women professing godliness. But to what extravagant, unbecoming, unnatural, repulsive, exorbitant, and shameless excesses many women of the present day adorn their person, every one who has powers of observation may readily perceive. How decidedly the apostle forbids women to adorn themselves with braided hair; yet it is lamentable to see to what inordinate excess many of the present day ornament their person, not only with braided hair, but also with gold, flowers, and plumes, together with many other odious and repulsive superfluities.

Hence, if such adornings as above described are not clear evidence of pride, I know no marks by which pride may be known to exist. Are not such persons intoxicated with pride? I think there is but little sobriety manifested in the deportment of such persons; but what pride, what ostentation is displayed! Each one desires to be "the greatest." Should, then, the writings of the holy and highly enlightened apostle be of no force in this our day? They no doubt wrote as they were moved by the Holy Ghost, and what they wrote against the adornments of the body we must receive as though it were spoken by God himself, for Paul said to the Corinthians (1 Cor. 14:37) that they should acknowledge that the things which he writes unto them *are the commandments of the Lord.* To the Romans (Rom. 12:2) he says, "Be not conformed to this world." Is it then, not in one respect at least, a conformity to the world, to adorn one's person in gorgeous and splendid apparel? Again he says (ver. 16), "Mind not high things, but condescend to men of low estate." Accordingly, then, there are (as we also know) two classes of people on the earth: the one low, and the other high; and to the former class the apostle exhorts the Romans to keep themselves. Now, dear reader, which seems to you to be the low class? Is it those who dress in a plain and simple manner; or those who dress in the highest fashions of the world and with outward adorning of the person? Does not sound reason teach that it is the former of these two classes? And where are "high things" chiefly to be found? Is it among the low, or the high class of men? The Savior also says, "That which is highly esteemed among men, is abomination in the sight of God."[17] Now, what is more highly es-

---

17   Luke 16:15b.

teemed among men, generally, than costly and splendid apparel? Let your conscience answer. Alas! why is earth and ashes proud?

We might quote from the Scriptures many more passages testifying against outward adornment, but I think that a sufficient number has been quoted to convince those that believe the Scriptures and wish to live in obedience to them. And, now, dear reader, will you still maintain that there is no ground in Scripture for insisting on simplicity of dress? Or is it a matter of no consequence in what manner we dress? Commonly those who oppose simplicity of apparel are such as themselves like to make a conspicuous appearance and set a high value on gorgeous styles of apparel. But he, whose heart still has pride within it, is also incapable of judging properly in this matter.

It is said that "the Hebrew name for garment is derived from a term signifying, *he has been unfaithful*. Thus our clothes are in fact nothing more nor less than a remembrancer of sin, reminding us of the first transgression. Is it not then a foolish ostentation, to seek honor in that which is but a memorial of our transgression by which we have lost the image of God? It is just as though a thief, having received pardon, but being obliged to wear a rope around his neck as a memorial of his theft, should seek to make a display of the same."[18]

But I would not by any means undertake to describe a form or pattern how our garments should be made, except that they should be plain and simple according to God's word. Christianity does not forbid the wearing of good, warm, comfortable, and clean clothes; but if the clothes are changed into a different style almost every year, and the outward person decorated and adorned with vain and useless things which neither serve to protect against heat and cold, nor afford the body either comfort or profit, but which are much rather injurious, and used only for display and in imitation of the wicked world; I must believe that these are certainly clear evidence, that pride is still existing in the heart.

David says, "Though the Lord be high, yet hath he respect unto the lowly; but the proud he knoweth afar off," Ps. 138:6. "Better

18   I have not been able to identify the source from which Brenneman is quoting. The claim regarding the Hebrew word for *garment* is incorrect; it does not derive from any term related to unfaithfulness. (Lee Anderson Jr., personal communication with editor, April 2018.)

is it to be of a humble spirit with the lowly than to divide the spoil with the proud," Prov. 16:19. If we are of a lowly mind, it will be altogether unnatural for us to aspire after high things.

Then, dear brethren and sisters, is it not greatly to be deplored that this fearful vice, pride, has been so extensively prevalent among us, and, like a contagious disease, is carrying off such vast numbers? Daily we see it increasing and men seeking only great honors in the world. Can we thus gain heaven? Oh! could we but take to heart St. John's admonition: "Love not the world, neither the things of the world. If any man love the world the love of the Father is not in him. For all that is in the world, the lust of the flesh, and the lust of the eyes, and the pride of life, is not of the Father, but is of the world,"[19] &c. Do we not see but too plainly the "pride of life" holding many of the so called Mennonites under its sway? And is this not a clear evidence of lukewarmness in religion? But God has plainly threatened such to spue them out of his mouth.

Happy is the man who can in truth say with David, "Lord, my heart is not haughty, nor mine eyes lofty," Ps. 131:1. There are, however, many at the present day, whose outward manner of dress is altogether uncensurable; but when we come into their houses, and there behold on all sides the evidence of pride and extravagance, and see their children dressed in the highest fashions of the world, we cannot possibly believe that they are indeed "lowly in heart," or that they really hate pride and wantonness. "The fear of the Lord is to hate evil: pride, and arrogancy, and the evil way, and the froward mouth, do I hate," Prov. 8:13.

No one will believe that I have a humble heart, however humble and plain my outward appearance may be, so long as I permit all manner of wantonness to be freely indulged in by my family, bringing my children up from infancy in the most wanton and shameless fashions of the world, and thus offering them a sacrifice to the haughty prince of darkness! We are equally responsible whether bringing up our own children, or those only that may have been committed to our care and training. It would be an utterly vain and useless excuse for any one to say that the children he has in his care are not his own, but have been only adopted.

---

19   1 John 2:15-16.

Pride in family members

Frequently, however, it may also be the case that, when the father wishes to admonish his children to modesty in dress, on account of his abhorrence to the wanton fashions of the world, the mother secretly encourages and aids them in their evil purposes, urging the father to indulge the children, and saying, "Oh let them alone, these and those have such things, and it is too hard that ours cannot have them," &c.; as if it were a hard matter, if the children are not brought up in pride such as Satan desires, or as if the word of God, testifying against pride, made a hard demand. The "wicked and slothful servant" said, "Lord, I knew thee that thou art a hard man," Matt. 25:24.

Mothers have a very great influence over their children and may aid much in keeping them under Christian discipline and instruction; but, on the other hand, they may, by their evil example, be instrumental in promoting their ruin. One would hardly think that there are to be found mothers professing Christianity who keep on hand two styles of clothing; the one fashionable and the other plain; the latter to put on when they attend public worship, and the other, when they go among the higher and fashionable classes. What is to be the end of such hypocrites is plainly to be seen in the word of God. "Whosoever will be a friend of the world is the enemy of God."[20] And "no man can serve two masters."[21] The end of the enemies of the cross of Christ is destruction, Phil. 3:10.

O fathers and mothers, let us, for God's sake, fulfill our duty towards our children: they are precious gifts committed by God to our care, of which we will have to give an account.

Some parents indeed pretend to assert that, when children have grown up and come to mature age, they will naturally see the folly of these things and put away the superfluous apparel. But it is manifest and easy to see, that, if they are permitted to have their own free will from their infancy up, to indulge in all the fashions of the world, this vice, pride, will thus have become so deeply rooted in them, that it will be far more difficult to induce them to renounce it, than if they had been accustomed from their youth

---

20   James 4:4b.
21   Matthew 6:24a.

up to a plain and simple mode. Too often it is the case, that when they have their own free will (which is naturally prone to evil) from their youth up, on arriving at mature age, they commonly go with the majority, where their corrupt nature can have its own free will without restraint.

And the men also. . .

And now, brethren, I would ask you out of love since women are so plainly and expressly forbidden, to adorn their person with plaiting of hair, gold, pearls, and costly array, whence then have the brethren any right to decorate their person with all manner of needless ostentation, trimming, combing, and disfiguring the hair after the silly fashions of the world? and such things, alas! are often to be seen even on your yet innocent little babes on your knees. Do you not consider what Jesus endured, on whose head our sins have inflicted such great sufferings? How then, can you still say, after being admonished to abandon such vain customs, but still persisting in them, that you are "clothed with humility"? or that you are "kindly affected one to another with brotherly love"[22]? Is not your insubordination to be regarded as a clear proof that pride is still lurking in your hearts? Oh! that every brother and sister would sincerely take to heart Paul's admonition, "Obey them that have the rule over you, and submit yourselves."[23]

Pride is also further plainly manifested in our day by the manner in which the beard is worn by many, and whether the brethren are all entirely guiltless in this respect or not, they themselves no doubt best know. I entreat you to examine yourselves in this matter; for God knows your hearts. I would however, not despise a modest or simple beard worn from pure motives and to the honor of God. We clearly find in Scripture that it was customary among the Jews. I have also read a poem written by Menno Simon in which he mentions the shaving off of the beard as a mark of antichrist.[24] Be this however as it may, we know that if we let our

---

22   Romans 12:10a.

23   Hebrews 13:24.

24   Brenneman appears to be referring to *Ausbund* #102, attributed to "M.S." Brenneman seems to have taken these initials to refer to Menno Simons, whereas they actually refer to Michael Schneider. Stanza 10 reads, "A part of his hair he [the Antichrist] has shorn, balding the top of his head. This has God, however,

Men can take pride in growing fashionable beards.

beards grow through pride and in order to conform to the world (which, I fear, is the case with many persons), we, without doubt, commit sin thereby. But if we do so through humility and to the honor of God, it will, no doubt, be pleasing to him. If, then, the beard is to be worn in humility and to the glory of God (Paul says, Whatsoever ye do, do all to the glory of God[25]), we must also conform to humility in our manner of wearing the hair on our heads and of dressing; otherwise it would only be hypocrisy. I think it is always easy to discern by a man's outward walk and conduct (especially by his manner of dressing) from what motives he wears his beard. I do not maintain that eternal salvation can be obtained by these plain modes of dress; but I do maintain that a humble heart no longer desires these useless, gaudy, and fashionable decorations, and that we ought to be able to distinguish, at

with His clear Word, forbidden man to do, nor should one cut off his beard. But this he [Antichrist] does not obey, he does the opposite, just as he wants, saying that it pleases God." *Songs of the Ausbund Volume II*, Ohio Amish Library, 2011, p. 309. This refers to the grooming of Roman Catholic monks.
25   1 Corinthians 10:31.

least, the humble Christian from the proud world, in general, by his outward deportment.

Therefore, ye watchmen of Zion, let us be mindful of our duty in this our important calling, that we warn the people in due season. Is it not to be feared that the watchmen are oftentimes in fault that this detestable vice has made such havoc in our churches, on account of their too great slothfulness in warning the people? Let us, therefore, "reprove, rebuke, exhort with all long-suffering and doctrine,"[26] wherever we see that it is necessary, "whether they will hear or whether they will forbear."[27] Let us cry aloud and not spare, and lift up our voices like a trumpet, and show the people their transgressions and their sins (Is. 58:1), lest we be found to be like those watchmen described in Is. 56:10. I fear that the reason why the watchmen are "dumb" and cannot reprove, is because so much evidence of pride is still found existing in their own houses, in themselves, and in their families. Oh! that we might not be of those who preach to others and are themselves cast away. "If a man know not how to rule his own house, how shall he take care of the church of God?" 1 Tim. 3:5. Many perhaps cannot reprove also "for filthy lucre's sake,"[28] lest their wages be thereby lessened.

Whosoever will indulge in this vice, cannot escape punishment. For "every one that is proud in heart is an abomination to the Lord: though hand join in hand, he shall not be unpunished," Prov. 16:5. "A man's pride shall bring him low," and God "hath scattered the proud in the imagination of their hearts," Luke 1:5. Yes, he resisteth them, which we will now secondly consider.

God, who is greater than all; who is the Creator of Heaven and earth, the sea and all that is in them, things visible and invisible; by whom the "things which are seen were not made of things which do appear;"[29] who stretches out the heavens like a curtain; to whom there is nothing impossible; who is omnipresent and omniscient – this incomprehensible, great God "resisteth the proud." Though the proud often resist God, yet they cannot succeed, even though they should all conspire together; for "all that are incensed

---

26 2 Timothy 4:2b.
27 Ezekiel 2:5, 7; 3:11.
28 Titus 1:11.
29 Hebrews 11:3b.

against him shall be ashamed," Isa. 45:24. Yea, God will make all the proud (who are his enemies) finally "his footstool."[30] He will subdue the proud and highminded, and be victorious over them; for if he is against them, who can be for them? God has at all times resisted the proud: proud Satan he cast out of heaven.

He resisted our first parents after they had transgressed his command. He imposed on them their punishment, and "placed at the east of the garden of Eden cherubim, and a flaming sword which turned every way, to keep the way of the tree of life."[31] When Cain rose up against his brother Abel and slew him, God said to him, "Now art thou cursed from the earth. When thou tillest the ground, it shall not henceforth yield unto thee her strength: a fugitive and vagabond shalt thou be in the earth."[32] This, I think, was a resistance. But when men began to multiply on the face of the earth and would no longer be reproved by the Spirit of God, taking them wives of whom they choose (which is still too often done) and their wickedness was great in the earth, and every imagination of the thoughts of their hearts was only evil continually, and God saw that all flesh had corrupted its way upon the earth, and the end of their time had come, then did he resist them with a flood and destroy them from off the face of the earth. Those only were saved that were in the ark. And in the course of time, when men again multiplied, and, as it seems, through pride desirous of making themselves a name, began to build a city, and a tower whose top might reach heaven, the Lord again resisted them by coming down and confounding their language, by which means he "scattered them abroad from thence upon the face of all the earth,"[33] and caused them to leave off to build the city.

Pride in Biblical history

The people of Sodom and Gomorrah doubtless were also a very proud people, whom God resisted by raining fire and brimstone out of heaven upon them and laying them in ashes.

King Pharaoh, who must also have been a very proud man, in that he greatly oppressed the Israelites in Egypt, God punished

---

30   Psalm 110:1; Hebrews 10:13.
31   Genesis 3:24.
32   Genesis 4:11-12.
33   Genesis 11:8.

with many plagues, and when he pursued Israel to the Red Sea with a large army God resisted them with a pillar of fire and finally destroyed him with his whole army in the Red Sea.

When Miriam spoke against Moses, as though he had assumed too much importance or authority, and, as it seems, she desired to be promoted herself, God also resisted and punished her, and she "became leprous, white as snow," Num. 12.

The Lord withstood also the proud and mutinous faction of Korah, Dathan, and Abiram, when he caused the earth to open her mouth and swallow them up, so that they and all that appertained to them went down alive into the pit, Num. 16. God visited Goliath by the hand of David.

And what was the fate of proud Haman, of whom we read in the book of Esther? When he rose up against Mordecai, and caused a gallows to be erected to hang him thereon, he himself was hung thereon.

In a peculiar manner did God resist king Nebuchadnezzar whose mind was hardened in pride. He was driven from men, and was wet with the dew of heaven, and did eat grass like oxen, till he knew that the Most High ruleth in the kingdom of men, and giveth it to whomsoever he will, Dan. 4. His son Belshazzar God also resisted on account of his pride, Dan. 5.

God also resisted the haughtiness of Herod, because he gave not God the honor, and he was smitten by the angel of the Lord and was eaten of worms, Acts. 12:23.

It would require too much time and space to mention all the instances that might be adduced on this point. Of Capernaum Jesus said, "And thou, Capernaum, which art exalted unto heaven, shalt be brought down to hell."[34] The proud Jews, who would not have Jesus to reign over them, and would not believe his words of Salvation, could not escape the resisting power of God's almighty hand. Their city and their temple were destroyed, and multitudes of them perished by the sword, by famine, and by pestilence, and those that remained were scattered into all countries and nations.

Thus we see that God has, from the beginning of the world, resisted the proud, and will continue to resist them until he has subdued or destroyed them. What is it else than pride, that keeps so

---

34   Matthew 11:23.

many thousands of persons from yielding obedience to the gospel of God? But God resists them with various plagues; as war, famine, pestilence, earthquakes, sickness, and punishments in various ways too numerous to be recounted here. And "he that, being often reproved, hardeneth his neck, shall suddenly be destroyed, and that without remedy," Prov. 29:1.

He will resist them also at the great judgment-day, when he shall be revealed from heaven "in flaming fire taking vengeance on them that know not God, and that obey not the gospel of our Lord Jesus Christ: who shall be punished with everlasting destruction."[35] When they shall see Abraham, Isaac, and Jacob, and all the prophets sitting in the kingdom of heaven, they will be cast out into outer darkness, where there shall be weeping and gnashing of teeth. Then he will say, "Depart from me, ye cursed, into everlasting fire prepared for the devil and his angels."[36] At that day "all the proud, yea, and all that do wickedly shall be stubble: and the day that cometh shall burn them up, saith the Lord of hosts, that it shall leave them neither root nor branch," Mal. 4:1. The proud will then no longer be able to stand before God, and will then "say to the mountains and rocks, fall on us, and hide us from the face of him that sitteth on the throne, and from the wrath of the Lamb: for the great day of his wrath is come, and who shall be able to stand?"[37] Oh, how fearful it will be for all the proud and high-minded to fall into the hands of almighty God! All ye proud, "repent, therefore, and be converted, that your sins may be blotted out."[38] Not all, I suppose, that may read these words of admonition will assent to all I have said; but I do not in the least fear that a single person of truly humble heart will become offended, or disaffected, thereby; and though it may be a cause of offense to the proud, yet we know that these were also offended at the saying of the Savior. I am, however, glad that I am not alone, but that there are many brethren who are of like mind with me and have encouraged me to attack this monstrous vice; and I hope they will still sustain and aid me in it.

---

35   2 Thessalonians 1:8-9a.
36   Matthew 25:41.
37   Revelation 6:16-17.
38   Acts 3:19.

Humility

We will now consider the latter and more agreeable part of our text, "and giveth grace to the humble."

The humble man feels small, poor, bowed, cast down, and unworthy within himself, and esteems others more highly than himself. He never boasts or exalts himself or despises others, as did the proud and conceited Pharisee; but much rather laments his weakness, his failings, and imperfections. He "minds not high things, but condescends to men of low estate."[39] He does not conform to this world in all manner of empty pomp, and pride, and sinful wantonness. He is usually of a quiet, meek, and gentle disposition, knowing when to be silent and when to speak. He is at all times willing to give place and opportunity to others to express their opinions. In company he observes due modesty, and does not seat himself in the most honorable, but much rather in the lowest place at table. In his deeds, actions, and pursuits, he does not indulge in vain ostentation: his utensils, furniture, and apparel in general being simple and modest, free from useless ornament and decoration; for he feels no pleasure or gratification in such outward splendor; but much rather dissatisfaction, disgust, and abhorrence, knowing that such things are sinful, transient, and vain; and he strives rather to secure the inward ornamenting of the soul by the putting on of the spiritual and divine virtues.

In their corrupt nature, men are generally not humble; but they are more or less disposed to pride from their youth up, which is very displeasing to God. Though they were in the beginning created good and noble in the image of God, exalted and set over all other creatures, yet, by their fall through transgression, they became the poorest and most wretched of all creatures, and notwithstanding their depraved and dangerous state they still frequently imagine that all is well with them, whilst they are even miserable, poor, "blind and naked."[40] But God is too merciful to leave them in this wretched condition without help: he is calling, reproving, and convincing them through his Spirit and other means of grace, in order to awaken them from their sleep of sin; and as soon as a man hears and truly heeds this calling voice, and being convicted,

---

39   Romans 12:16b.
40   Revelation 3:17.

sees that he is a poor, lost, and guilty sinner, and feels that his sins are a burden to him too heavy to be borne, he becomes so much oppressed and bowed down by this burden that he becomes small and poor within himself. Such a person feels then like David, who exclaimed, "I am bowed down greatly; I go mourning all the day long. All the night make I my bed to swim; I water my couch with my tears."[41] He feels as though he were the poorest and unworthiest of all men. Nay, he thinks he is no more worthy to be called a son or a child. He is glad to be reckoned as one of the least, or as a hireling. He can then, and will with a true heart, like the poor publican, smite his breast and pray, "God, be merciful to me a sinner;"[42] or, like David, "create in me a clean heart, O God; and renew a right spirit within me."[43] A man, thus truly penitent and humble in heart, truly turning to God, sincerely seeking him day and night in prayer and supplication, wholly offering himself in sacrifice to him, humbly submitting to his powerful hand, and desirous henceforth to live unto him and continue faithful in his service to the end – such a man is, in the Scriptures, called a humble man; and such are they to whom God gives *grace*; as, for example, the woman who was a sinner, and humbled herself at the feet of Jesus, washing them with tears and wiping them with the hairs of her head, unto whom he said, "thy sins are forgiven. Thy faith hath saved thee: go in peace."[44] All such penitent and humble sinners, seeking grace, shall obtain it of God through Jesus Christ. For "where sin abounded, *grace* did much more abound."[45] "*Grace* and truth came by Jesus Christ,"[46] and "of his fullness have all we received, and *grace* for *grace*,"[47] says John. Grace is, therefore, the opposite of merit; for when a man gives me that which he owes me, and which I have earned by labor, he gives it to me, not out of grace, but out of indebtedness. But if any one bestows on me good gifts, which I have not merited and which he does not owe me, he bestows them on me purely out of

---

41   Psalm 38:6; Psalm 6:6b-c.
42   Luke 18:13.
43   Psalm 51:10.
44   Luke 7:48, 50.
45   Romans 5:20b.
46   John 1:17b.
47   John 1:16.

Abase and humble yourself as did the penitent publican,
and you will also obtain mercy for your poor soul.

grace. Such a person, therefore, I might call gracious, inasmuch
as he has bestowed on me his grace or made me a partaker of his
grace; that is, he has given or granted me grace. In like manner
God has made us partakers of his grace, for he does not owe us
any thing; but on the other hand we owe him ten thousand pounds,
and have not one farthing with which to pay this great debt. But
God will remit it out of pure *grace*, if we but with true penitence
of heart humble ourselves before him and confess our sins before
him, feel sorry on account of them, and from our heart pray to him
in the name of Jesus for pardon; then "he *giveth grace*"[48] to us.
It is through grace, therefore, that such humble, penitent sinners
are saved, and made "accepted" through his dear Son. "And if
by grace, then is it no more of works: otherwise grace is no more
grace," Rom. 11:6. Through grace we are regenerated, and born
anew, and accepted through Jesus Christ as children, and made
heirs of his eternal and heavenly kingdom; that is *"he giveth grace
to the humble."* He gives grace to them even in this life, inasmuch
as he pardons their sins and blesses them in body and soul with all
manner of good gifts; and in the life to come he bestows on them
eternal and heavenly gifts and possessions, and eternal joy, rest,
and happiness. Oh how unspeakably great is this promise, "He

---

48   Proverbs 3:34; James 4:6.

giveth grace to the humble!" For the grace of God is of ten thousand times greater value than the whole world with all its pleasure, pomp, honor, and glory can ever be. "My grace is sufficient for thee,"[49] he said to Paul – as much as to say, "My grace supplies all your wants: you have need of nothing more." I believe sincerely that whoever cannot content himself with the sufficiency of God's grace can never have any real enjoyment; for the grace of God is sufficient for us in time and in eternity. If we are partakers of his grace and confide in it, we have all that we need in order to become happy, glorified and blessed in this world and in the world to come; and what more can we wish? But bear in mind, this grace is given only to the *humble*. O humility, noble virtue! how needful it is! It is worth more than gold and wealth, and worldly glory. Without humility we have no promise of the saving power of grace; and without this saving grace no one can be a child, and consequently cannot be an heir of God. O how necessary it is that we candidly examine ourselves whether we are in possession of this indispensable virtue, since on humility alone is bestowed this promise of grace. Without true humility of heart we have no promise of grace; but on the contrary we are threatened with God's resistance, and his threatenings stand equally as firm as his promises; for the words of Jesus are firm and unchangeable. "Every one that exalteth himself (like the proud Pharisee) shall be abased, and he that humbleth himself (like the publican) shall be exalted."[50]

Reasons to humble ourselves

We have great cause to humble ourselves: *First*, on account of our sins, through which we have separated ourselves from God, who is so good, so holy, and so kind. O sin, what a detestable vice! It should cause us to bow down, to humble ourselves in the dust, and with shame to repent in sack-cloth and ashes. Oh! that we were not so obstinate and stiffnecked, and would no longer hesitate to humble ourselves and to bow under the mighty hand of God, since we are nothing at all without his grace. Will we then wantonly continue to sin against the grace of God, since we have not for one

---

49   2 Corinthians 12:9.
50   Luke 18:14b.

moment any security of our life? Oh how great the long-suffering of God toward man, since he does not desire that any one should be lost, but that every one should repent of his sins, confess them, amend his life, and *humble himself.*

Secondly, we have cause to humble ourselves, because Christ has commanded it. "Seek righteousness, seek *humility*: it may be you shall be hid in the day of the Lord's anger," Zeph. 2:3. "He hath showed thee, O man, what is good; and what doth the Lord require of thee, but to do justly, and love mercy, and to walk *humbly* with thy God?" Mic. 6:8. "Humble yourselves under the mighty hand of God," 1 Pet. 5:6. "In lowliness of mind let each esteem other better than themselves," Phil. 2:3. "Walk worthy of the vocation wherewith ye are called, with all lowliness and meekness, with longsuffering, forbearing one another in love," Eph. 4:1, 2. "Be clothed with humility," 1 Pet. 5:5.

Thirdly, on account of God's precious promises. "He giveth grace to the humble." He has also promised to dwell with them. "For thus saith the high and lofty One that inhabiteth eternity, whose name is Holy; I dwell in the high and holy place, with him also that is of a contrite and humble spirit, to revive the spirit of the humble, and to revive the heart of the contrite ones," Isa. 57:15. "He shall save the humble person," Job 22:29. "With the lowly is wisdom," Prov. 11:2. "Honor shall uphold the humble in spirit," Prov. 29:23. "He that humbleth himself shall be exalted," Luke 18:14.

Fourthly, the threatenings of God. "He resisteth the proud." "He hath scattered the proud in the imaginations of their hearts," Luke 1:51. "Every one that is proud in heart is an abomination to the Lord: he shall not be unpunished," Prov. 16:5. "A man's pride shall bring him low," Prov. 29:23. "Every one that exalteth himself shall be abased," Luke 18:14. "Be not high-minded, but fear: for if God spared not the natural branches, take heed lest he also spare not thee."[51]

Fifthly, the example of Jesus Christ. He is "meek and lowly in heart."[52] Behold, what an unparalleled example of humility he has left us, when he, the Lord of lords and King of kings, washed

---

51   Romans 11:20b-21.
52   Matthew 11:29.

his disciples' feet! How condescendingly our Lord and Master stooped and humbled himself. Greater humility, it seems to me, could not have been manifested than Jesus manifested on this occasion. He also said, "If I, then, your Lord and Master, have washed your feet, ye also ought to wash one another's feet. For I have given you an example, that ye should do as I have done to you."[53] Are we, then, all perfectly willing thus to stoop and to humble ourselves in conformity to the example of Jesus? Oh, how many Christian professors there are who refuse to do this! We should not, however, when we wash one another's feet, expect thereby to gain our salvation, nor is it for the purpose of washing away outward impurity from the feet; but simply to show *obedience, love, and humility*; and to show that we are not ashamed of Jesus and of his words. For, if we perform merely the outward act of washing one another's feet, and have not a genuine *humility of heart* and sincere love towards each other, we shall not in the least be benefitted by it; but rather thereby bring on ourselves greater sin. In *lowliness of mind* we should each esteem another better than himself. The richest and most highly esteemed should not think himself too good to stoop and wash the feet of the least and the poorest member. If Jesus had bid us do "some great thing,"[54] would we not do it? How much rather, then, since he has said, "Ye also ought to wash one another's feet,"[55] inasmuch as he has given an example that we should do as he has done; and says, "Learn of me; for I am meek and lowly in heart."[56]

"He humbled himself and became obedient unto death, even the death of the cross," Phil. 2:8. Oh! consider then. For if Jesus, the Lord of Heaven, thus stooped and humbled himself, took on him the form of a servant, was spit upon, scourged, and crucified for us, to reconcile us and to redeem us from the curse and from death; how it becomes us, to imitate his example and to follow his footsteps in humility!

---

53   John 13:14-15.
54   2 Kings 5:13.
55   John 13:14.
56   Matthew 11:29.

Which will we choose?

Now, dear readers, having seen the great difference between the proud and the humble, what will we do? The former God resists, but he gives grace to the latter. Which, then, will we choose? God's grace, or to be resisted by him? I hope we will choose his grace. Though it is not otherwise to be obtained than by passing through the valley of humiliation,[57] let us not on that account be frightened back; but truly bend and humble ourselves. Remember, Jesus was humble, he did not exalt himself. O, what should we not, therefore, willingly do, to obtain the grace of God? We should humble ourselves before him with fasting, with weeping, and fervent prayer, till he hears us and gives us grace. My brethren and sisters, allow me to speak freely to you. In what condition do we find ourselves? Are we humble at heart? It will not profit us in the least, if we only assume an outward, dissembling[58] form of humility, without genuine and unfeigned humility of heart; for this alone is valid in the sight of God. "For the Lord seeth not as man seeth; for man looketh on the outward appearance, but the Lord looketh on the heart," 1 Sam. 16:7. Yea, he is a Searcher of hearts, and all our thoughts are open to his sight and known to him. But if we are truly humble in heart, then, without doubt, "that which is highly esteemed among men," and which "is abomination in the sight of God," will also be abomination to us. For, if we are truly humble, we have also obtained his grace; and if we have his grace, we have also his Spirit; and if we have his Spirit, we are also his children; and if we are his children, we are also partakers of his divine nature; and, if we are partakers of his divine nature, it is indisputably true that "that which is highly esteemed among men," and which "is abomination in the sight of God,"[59] must also be abomination to us. Let us, then, candidly as in the sight of God examine whether we do not still take too much pleasure in those things which are highly esteemed among men. God the Searcher of our hearts knows what is in them: we cannot deceive him. "Be not deceived; God is not mocked."[60]

---

57   An allusion to John Bunyan's *Pilgrim's Progress*.
58   Deceptive, hypocritical.—*AVS*.
59   Luke 16:15b.
60   Galatians 6:7a.

However humble we may appear outwardly, yet as long as we approve of the needless and vain ornamenting and decorating of our houses and our families, and do not use our utmost diligence to prevent and to do away with such abominations, I cannot possibly believe that "that which is highly esteemed among men," is abomination to us; and if such vain and worldly aspirations have not yet become abominations to us, we have not yet been made partakers of the divine nature, and consequently cannot be children of God; for the children of God partake of the nature and character of God, which no one can deny. Oh! who should not seriously reflect on it, when beholding the wickedness and pride of the world. The majority seem to hurry willfully with the great tide of worldly ambition on the broad road to the abyss of ruin. How frightfully they pervert their being, so that they scarcely appear like human beings. It seems that they are not satisfied any more with the form which God gave them. We are forced to think of many, that they do not fear God, nor regard man.

Should this now come before the eyes or ears of any one who finds himself sunk and enveloped in the wickedness of pride, I would say to him: "Haste! haste! and deliver your precious soul: flee out of Babel! Flee! Flee, I pray you, out of the Sodom of this perverse and sinful world, that you be not partakers of its plagues. Oh! forsake hastily the broad road of vice, and humble yourself under the mighty hand of God, before it is forever too late. Oh! repent quickly and be converted that your sins may be blotted out. Abase and humble yourself as did the penitent publican, and you will also obtain mercy for your poor soul. Seek grace in humility and not in pride; for again I say unto you, '*God giveth grace to the humble,*' and not to the proud. Oh! come, then, I entreat you, every one who may read or hear this, if you have not already come. Hearken, ye can still find grace: come all things are ready. 'Come boldly unto the throne of grace, that you may obtain mercy, and find grace to help in time of need.'[61] Come now and do not wait for a 'more convenient season.'[62] 'Look diligently, lest any man fail of the grace of God.' Heb. 12:15. 'The Spirit and the bride say, Come. And let him that heareth say, Come. And let him that

---

61   Hebrews 4:16.
62   Acts 24:25.

is athirst come. And whosoever will, let him take the water of life freely.'[63]"

I feel as though I could hardly cease to warn you, O wretched man! Examine yourself seriously and critically by the mirror here placed before you, and consider well what is your character and to which class you belong, whether to the proud or the humble. Oh! examine yourself: it is not a small matter. You may soon, very soon and unexpectedly, be removed from this world, to receive the rewards of God's eternal grace, or to receive "indignation and wrath, tribulation and anguish,"[64] which shall be to "every soul of man that doeth evil."[65] If you find yourself still in the way of the proud, turn, oh! turn, and have compassion on yourself, O man! and be admonished that the indignation of God be not your eternal lot. Permit yourself, I entreat you, to be persuaded.

Conclusion

In conclusion, I hope my readers will receive in love my humble exhortation, and examine it closely, and if they find the truth therein brought before them, I wish they might heartily embrace the cause and assist me to contend against pride, and to inculcate humility. Especially would I wish to invite my fellow-laborers to take the privilege and opportunity, to make further remarks on this subject, to improve or supply what is needed to fill up any deficiency that may yet exist. I wish with my whole heart to all the readers the saving grace of God, the love of Jesus, and the communion of the Holy Ghost. But know, I say again, that God gives this grace *only to the humble*. May he make this exhortation a blessing to many hearts, that they may thereby be brought to reflect, and in humility to turn to God, if they have not already done so, and to entreat him for grace while grace is yet offered, that he alone may thereby be honored through Jesus Christ. Amen.

---

63   Revelation 22:17.
64   Romans 2:8b-9a.
65   Romans 2:9b.

"A sword against the enemy, is humbleness of heart;
From him who hath a humble mind he quickly must depart:
His haughty, proud, ferocious mien humility disdains
He cannot even think to be where meekness humbly reigns:
It wounds him—cuts him to the heart—to see a humble mind.
Because his nature's haughty, proud—quite otherwise inclined."

An Alarm to the Proud

"Let sudden fear come upon you, ye proud women, tremble ye careless ones; the time of stripping off, making bare and girding of the loins is at hand," Isa. 32:11.[1]

Before the fall, man was a very happy and noble creature, for he was made after the image and in the likeness of God. After the fall he was the very poorest and most miserable of all creatures; for now, in his deeply fallen condition, he was separated from God, the source of all good, and would eternally have had to remain separated from him, had not God, out of love, grace and mercy, given his beloved Son as our Redeemer, Mediator and Reconciler, through whom man can again become united and obtain peace with God. There are however too few of mankind who are willing to be brought to God through Jesus Christ the dear Redeemer, for man is, in his fallen, carnal condition, so contrary, depraved and blind, and disinclined to all that is good, that he is not willing to be taught, aided or directed. Yea he often imagines that he is rich and has need of nothing; and generally in himself he is so conceited, proud and haughty that he imagines himself much better and nobler than other persons, and hence often exalts himself above his fellow-men, and only makes sport of them and despises them. The Psalmist says, "The wicked through the pride of his countenance will not seek after God; God is not in all his thoughts," Ps. 10:4. The Lord through the prophet Isaiah declares that he will cause the arrogancy of the proud to cease and lay low the haughtiness of the terrible, Isa. 13:11. "Every one that is proud in heart is an abomination to the Lord," Prov. 16:5. Amos says, "Woe to them which are at ease in Zion," according to the German translation, *Woe to the*

---

1   This text and its connections are here used according to the German translation.

proud in Zion, Amos 6:1. As we have already said, the proud are very lofty and conceited in themselves, which may very readily be seen in their conduct, appearance, gestures, words and actions. David says, "Him that hath a high look and a proud heart will not I suffer," Ps. 101:5.

The Scriptures speak and testify chiefly against pride among the female sex. In the first place this corrupting vice was implanted by the enemy of souls into our first mother Eve, and it seems as though he still, to the present time, has been able to propagate best this vile seed of all evil among the female sex. Pride and extravagance is frequently plainly visible among them in the costly show of their apparel, decoration and adornment, with which they seek to gain the love and respect of this sinful, wicked world, which however is highly displeasing unto God, and though men may manifest the pride of their hearts and self exaltation in different ways; many do so in an especial manner with the needless and sinful adornment of their bodies, which both Paul and Peter have forbidden, 1 Tim. 2:9, 1 Pet. 3:3-5. For this reason the Lord has severely threatened the daughters of Zion to take away their adornments, when he says, "Moreover the Lord saith, Because the daughters of Zion are haughty (proud), and walk with stretched forth necks and wanton eyes, walking and mincing as they go, and making a tinkling with their feet; therefore the Lord will smite with a scab the crown of the head of the daughters of Zion. . . . In that day the Lord will take away the bravery of their tinkling ornaments about their feet, and their cauls, and their round tires like the moon, the chains and the bracelets,"[2] &c. The words of our text seem to harmonize with this passage, "Let sudden fear come upon you, ye proud women, tremble ye careless ones, the time of stripping off, making bare and girding of the loins is at hand." Because they were proud, they no doubt also adorned themselves with unnecessary apparel; hence it was said to them, "the time of stripping off and making bare is at hand."

The merciful Father in heaven does not leave a single individual without his testimony, but through his servants, through his word and Spirit, as of old, he yet warns them. The prophet here directs his commission especially to the proud and secure women,

---

2   Isaiah 3:16-19.

and proclaims unto them the judgment of God which perhaps was not far distant. He gave them distinctly to understand that soon a dearth should come, in which their superabundance should be turned into penury and want. He speaks to them as follows, "Rise up ye proud women;[3] hear my voice ye careless daughters; give ear to my speech. Many days and years shall ye be troubled, ye careless women; for the vintage shall fail and gathering shall not come."[4] He shows them that a dearth shall come and therefore says further, "let sudden fear come upon you, ye proud women, tremble ye careless ones; the time of stripping off, making bare and girding of the loins is at hand." Perhaps in their future sorrow and trouble they would or should be brought to put on sackcloth, as the Prophet says, Isa. 15:3, "In their streets they shall gird themselves with sackcloth." "They shall lament for the teats, for the pleasant fields, for the fruitful vine. Upon the land of my people shall come thorns and briers," &c. Their fields should become a desert and unfruitful.

It is frequently the case that when men are blessed with temporal goods, and have all things in abundance, they become proud and careless towards God, yea, ungrateful, rich and feel not the need of anything. Therefore Paul writes not without some purpose to Timothy. "Charge them that are rich in this world that they be not high-minded."[5] Generally when men become rich they soon forget that God is the giver of every good and perfect gift, and it has always been the case, that when men once became so proud and careless, as if there was no danger, and forgot God, their Creator, he soon brought upon them his judgments, for the purpose of again bringing to their remembrance from whence such gifts proceed, and that they should be converted unto him, humble themselves and acknowledge that he is God over all. But generally before he brought his judgments upon them he first had them warned, so that they had no excuse when the judgments came upon them. Here also in our text we may see how earnestly and faithfully God warned the proud and careless women, through his prophet, who made known unto them the future judgment which

---

3   German translation.
4   Isaiah 32:9-10.
5   1 Timothy 6:17.

should come upon them. "Let sudden fear come upon you, ye proud women; tremble ye careless ones," says he, and also gives them a reason why they should do so, namely, the time of stripping off, making bare and girding of the loins, is at hand. The judgments of God upon you he desires to say, are at hand, in which your costly decorations and adornments will be stripped off; your riches and your over-abundance will be taken from you, and you shall be made bare and bald. When this should be accomplished they would say with Micah, "Ye have taken my gods, . . . and what have I more?"[6] He tells them too that a girding of the loins is at hand. They should perhaps be driven out of their goodly land by their enemies, or be compelled to flee in great haste. Hence they should gird their loins and be ready to hasten away, like the children of Israel when they fled from Egypt. So great should be the trouble that should come upon them that even at its proclamation by the prophet they should already be filled with sudden fear, and tremble.

Generally when men discover that they are in danger and that they are to be overtaken by sorrow and want, they will be terrified and tremble even as Belshazzar. When he saw the handwriting on the wall his countenance was changed and his thoughts troubled him, so that the joints of his loins were loosed and his knees smote one against another, Dan. 5:6. Or like Felix, when Paul reasoned before him of righteousness, of temperance and of judgment to come, he trembled. It was undoubtedly the judgment to come which caused him to tremble. And so also it was for the judgment which was at hand on account of which the proud women are called upon by the prophet, in our text, to fear and tremble. No doubt those who believed the word of God, spoken through the prophet, and sincerely repented and humbled themselves before him, obtained mercy, for we see how God, when he had threatened the Ninevites, saying, "Yet forty days and Nineveh shall be overthrown,"[7] spared them again when they repented. It is also written in the prophecy of Jeremiah, "At what instant I shall speak concerning a nation, and concerning a kingdom, to pluck up and to pull down, and to destroy it; if that nation against whom I have

---

6   Judges 18:24.
7   Jonah 3:4.

pronounced, turn from their evil, I will repent of the evil that I thought to do unto them," Jer. 18:7, 8.

Let us now apply this prophetical text to the women of the present day. I do not expect to obtain honor or praise thereby. If this had been my object I would have remained silent on this subject. And could we be saved by the praise and commendations of men, then this would, no doubt, also be acceptable to my own nature, which is ever yet too much inclined to sin. But "if I yet pleased men," says Paul, "I should not be the servant of Christ."[8] Notwithstanding I do not desire wantonly or unnecessarily to hurt the feelings of any person in the world, yet without doubt, my discourse will touch hard many women who have frequently manifested much love and friendship towards me, who have received me into their houses and treated me with great kindness while upon my journeyings, for which I also sincerely thank them, and pray God that he may reward them for it; but tell me, ye proud women, should I now for the love you manifested towards me, harden my heart against you and not point out to you the terrible danger in which you stand concerning your souls? If you together with your children should be lost through my unfaithfulness and carelessness, could you in eternity forgive me? Therefore I pray you, do not take it unkindly, if I seek to fulfill, faithfully, the will of my heavenly Father towards you, in order that I may be free from your blood, so that your souls, in the day of judgment may not be required of my hand as of a dumb watchman. This is my whole and only object, if in the least I know myself. If I should see either you or your children's life in danger and you did not know it, and I would not tell you, neither assist in saving you, when at the same time, I could easily do so, and harden my heart against you, would you not then think that I was unworthy the name of a man? If it were then to me so great a sin to value your physical life so low, how much more would it be a very great sin, to me to disregard your spiritual and eternal life for which Christ died!

My discourse, however, is not in any measure directed to the innocent and humble, but particularly to the proud, therefore "Let sudden fear come upon you, ye proud women, tremble ye careless ones; the time of stripping off and making bare, is at hand." Yea

---

8   Galatians 1:10b.

there is at hand a terrible judgment, for "Behold the Lord cometh with ten thousand of his saints to execute judgment."[9]—O there is at hand an eternal ruin, pain and torment; yea, an eternal fire, prepared for the devil and his angels, and it will also be the portion of all the proud, haughty and self-exalted women, if they do not sincerely repent, be converted to God and become regenerated in the day of grace. O! let me now yet warn you, "Repent and be converted that your sins may be blotted out."[10] Lay aside your vain adornments, even as the Lord commanded Israel, Ex. 3:5, and humble yourselves like the woman that was a sinner, who washed the feet of Jesus with tears, and ye may yet obtain grace, and escape the future judgment and eternal condemnation. Oh! haste that your poor souls may be saved, for soon it will be too late! Oh! tremble ye careless ones! Generally when a person sees no danger, and imagines all is secure around him, he feels and lives secure, but often amidst his supposed security he is in the greatest danger.

So it is also with the proud; they imagine there is no danger, and with this belief they feel entirely secure, and, poor mortals! they do not know which moment they may sink into perdition, "for what is your life?" says James, "it is even a vapor that appeareth for a little time and then vanisheth away."[11] "Verily," says David, "every man at his best estate is altogether vanity,"[12] but Solomon says, "He that walketh uprightly, walketh surely."[13] Who then can imagine that he is secure? Though he that truly feareth God, may say, "Behold God is my salvation; I will trust and not be afraid," Isa. 12:2. But the proud have the very greatest reason to fear, for there is at hand an indescribable danger, which is rapidly approaching and will surely overtake them.

Every Christian no doubt, will acknowledge with me, that it is not an overdrawn picture to apply the words of our text to the great majority of the women of the present day. For who can show us a time since the creation of the world, in which there was more pride, pomp and extravagance to be seen among the female sex

9   Jude 1:14b-15a.
10   Acts 3:19b.
11   James 4:14b.
12   Psalm 39:5b.
13   Proverbs 10:9a.

This illustration from *Gazette of Fashion* (1859) shows a fashionably-dressed couple with the woman in a hoop skirt.

than now? And all the preaching, admonishing, reproving, warning and writing against the abominable vice, seems to be well-nigh in vain; indeed, many it seems only to excite to laughter, and they go even so far as to make sport of those who, prompted by love and kindness, would speak to them words of warning. But God knows that I do not wish to go too far in this matter, or to exaggerate the sins which originate from pride and extravagance, or to represent them greater than they really are. How could the decorations of the body as displayed at present in dress be exceeded, especially among the female sex? And is this not a clear testimony that their hearts are filled with pride and self exaltation? If not, God would have wronged the daughters of Zion, when he threatened them, on account of their pride, to take away their adornments. If, however, this abominable adornment of dress was to be found only among the wicked children of the world, it would not be so surprising, but now there is scarcely any difference to be seen between those and most of the Christian professors. Is it not, then, enough to bring sudden fear upon a true Christian and cause him to tremble out of sympathy towards those poor, deluded people, especially towards his friends and relatives, when he sees the gay display of fashionable dressing? May we not fear that terrible judgments, such as famine, pestilence or earthquakes might be in store for our land and near at the door? It seems to me impossible that our kind heavenly Father could forbear much longer. For example, what could be more needless, inconvenient, unbecoming and immodest than hoop-skirts? It seems to me that this is the most disgraceful fashion that Satan ever invented, and it seems to please him the very best, for other fashions generally after a short time are laid aside again, but this still remains.[14]

Is it not dreadful to think that poor mortals allow themselves to be so tormented and burdened by Satan? Some have already lost their lives by these things, and of how many instances have we already seen and heard where women and maidens have mourned and lamented over themselves on their death-beds, on account of their pride and adornments, and ordered their hoops, ear-rings, and other such like vain ornaments to be burned? Oh! how often does conscience awake when persons are once laid upon their death-beds, when it is, perhaps, forever too late! Hence, "Let sudden fear come upon you, ye proud women," and do not imagine that you can be walking in the footsteps of Jesus on the strait and narrow way, while you adorn yourselves with hoops, feathers, flowers, jewelry and such like decorations. "Be not deceived; God is not mocked."[15]

Do not say that the writer is a person who seeks religion in his clothes, for he well knows that the clothes do not change any one's heart; but he maintains that when the heart of man is truly changed, regenerated and filled with the Holy Spirit, he will be satisfied with moderate and modest apparel, and that he will then no longer desire anything that is superfluous and highly esteemed by the world; but on the other hand, he will much more abhor them, and avoid all needless outward adornment and decoration of the body, because he knows that such things are displeasing to God, and forbidden in his word. The proud themselves often, upon their death-beds, give testimony against these things. Where is there a woman to be found who would not be filled with horror if she knew that after her death she should be buried in her hoop-skirts? and how can you follow Jesus with such abomina-

---

14   This article was written when hoop-skirts were still in fashion, and although they have now almost passed out of fashion, there are again in their stead things which are fully as bad and degrading.

15   Galatians 6:7a.

This Amish
family from
the 1800s shows
plainly-dressed
parents, but with
bows, collars, and
ruffles sprouting
on the children.

tions with which you would not even be buried? Oh! tremble ye
careless ones, and awake from the sleep of sin, and do not allow
yourselves to be so blinded by Satan, for he only seeks to sink
your souls into eternal fire.

Now also let sudden fear come upon you, oh! ye proud Mennonite women, for you are in the same danger as all other proud
women, and how should I be able to give an account of myself
if I should not earnestly warn you? What benefit will the name
"Mennonite" be to you, as long as you do not follow Jesus in the
regeneration! O! examine yourselves and see by which spirit you
are filled and led! Do you not know that "that which is highly
esteemed among men is abomination in the sight of God?"[16] I do
not know any Mennonite sisters that wear hoop-skirts, feathers,
or flowers, and oh! how glad would I feel if I could say the same
of all your daughters! Oh! think how painful it is for your poor
ministers, and how pitiful it appears to them when they come to
you (although you receive them in a friendly manner), and must
see your daughters with hoop-skirts, gay and flashy, short dresses,
and their hair cut off (which is directly against the teachings of
Paul, 1 Cor. 11), and otherwise following the vain fashions of the
world? Have we not, in such cases, reason to doubt, whether ye
yourselves are sincerely humble, or whether you are led by the
Spirit of God, or whether you have earnestly sought to bring up
your daughters in the fear and admonition of the Lord? Perhaps
you may say, they do not obey me. In that case I must reply that

16   Luke 16:15.

This 1859 illustration shows fashionable clothing for
women and girls.

no doubt in a great measure it must be your own fault; you have
put off your duty so long, and from childhood, you have too much
left them have their own way. Oh! tremble ye careless and inac-
tive women and mothers!

But are you followers and disciples of Jesus as you profess,
then for Jesus' sake, do not give up your daughters as being past
reclaiming. I pray you, warn them of hell and eternal condemnation while you have the opportunity to do so; warn them with all
earnestness and with tears, and seek to lead them to Jesus; pray for
them day and night "without ceasing"[17] like the woman of Canaan
did for her daughter, who was grievously vexed with a devil, and
obtained her request. Thus there are still to-day many daughters
vexed; therefore do not let them fall such an easy prey into the
hands of Satan, and without an effort to save them, for in eternity
it will be too late to do anything for them. Therefore do not neglect them, so that they may not on their death-beds or in the day
of judgment, accuse[18] you of your neglect and tell you that you

17 1 Thessalonians 5:17.
18 The original has "accurse." "Accuse" is probably meant.—*Ed.*

never warned them. Oh! how hard it will be for such careless mothers, or parents to give an account in the great day that awaits us all, who have not only not warned their children of the abominations of pride, but have yet helped them to it, and led them on therein, that they might not be despised and made sport of by the wicked world.

But tell me now ye mothers, would it not be ten thousand times better that they should be despised and made sport of here in this world and be united with Jesus, than to enjoy the honor and respect of the world for so short a time and be slaves of Satan, and then finally be eternally lost. No doubt you will answer affirmatively.

Menno Simon says, "I consider it unquestionably true that all true, believing parents are thus minded towards their children that they would far sooner see them scourged from head to feet, for the sake of the glory and the holy name of the Lord, than to see them adorn themselves with silks, velvets, gold, silver, costly, striped and fashionable clothes, and the like vanity, pomp and haughtiness." Page 150 Comp. Ed.

But how can we believe that such mothers which aid and assist their daughters to make such display in pride and extravagance and even lead them on in it, are true believing and humble Christians, or that they are led by the Spirit of Christ? The Spirit of God leads no one into pride, but much more into humility; neither does he lead any one to conform himself to the world, but rather to separate himself from it. If the mothers are truly humble and led by the divine Spirit, they will put forth earnest efforts to do the will of God, and his will is, that we should bring up our children in the nurture and admonition of the Lord. He that hath the Spirit of God (as his children have), which is the Spirit of love, loves all men, and desires to help them in seeking their salvation, and especially does he desire to do this with his children, and he that loveth them chasteneth them betimes, not in anger and revenge, but with love and meekness.

Oh! ye mothers to whom God hath given sons and daughters to bring up, for which you must give an account, "Let sudden fear come upon you and tremble" if you have until now neglected your duty towards them. Yes, I say, Let sudden fear come upon you, and consider your duty in the day of grace, while there yet is hope, so that you will not be compelled to tremble in vain before the judgment seat. If you should now see your daughters in danger of their lives, by fire or water, or any other cause, would you not use all your strength and every means in your power to save them? No doubt you will answer "yes;" and would you not consider her an inhuman mother that would not do this? Undoubtedly. Now then when you see your daughters walking with their terrible pride and vanity on the broad road that leadeth to the abyss of eternal fire, into hell and eternal damnation, where the worm dieth not and the fire is not quenched, how can it be possible, if the love of God through the Holy Spirit is shed abroad in your hearts, that you can remain silent and unconcerned, and not use all possible means to liberate your beloved daughters from the galling chains of Satan and save them from the eternal torments? O, would it not be acting unmercifully and inhumanly towards your daughters if you would not try to do something for them in this respect? Yet, notwithstanding it is to be feared that many mothers or parents show themselves thus unconcerned in regard to the eternal happiness of their children.

And Oh! you proud and careless young women, who are bound by Satan with the bonds of this abominable pride, do not reject these well-meant warnings and admonitions. Do you wish to be forever blessed and happy, then cast away all sinful display, adornment, and decoration; sincerely and earnestly repent and seek Jesus, who is so willing to save you. Pray to him with all earnestness that he may adorn and decorate you with the robe of righteousness on the inner man and with spiritual, holy virtues; yes, that he may adorn you with his holy image and be formed in you. This will be worth to you a thousand times more than all the outward adornments and decorations of the body. When your mothers admonish and warn you, and try to lead you away from pride and vain show, give ear to their instructions with a willing mind, and thank God that he has given you such pious mothers, who feel an interest in your eternal salvation. Oh! try to become truly humble, for in humility alone is Jesus to be found.

But if you believe and imagine that you may adorn and decorate yourselves after the customs of the fashionable world, conform yourselves to the world, and maintain the friendship of the world and after all be saved, depend upon it, Satan has blinded your eyes, and is trying to sink your poor souls into eternal perdition, therefore let sudden fear come upon you, and tremble ye careless ones! yea, fear and tremble, all ye careless ones whosoever and wheresoever you may be, "for the time of stripping off, making bare, and girding of the loins is at hand." Yea, there is at hand death and the day of judgment, when ye shall be stripped of all your outward adornments and decorations, and when you shall leave all your temporal possessions and treasures behind.

Oh! that in this day of grace a sincere spiritual stripping off and making bare might take place with all of us, that we might in good time lay off the old man and all self righteousness, and "put on the new man, which, after God, is created in righteousness and true holiness."[19] Then, no doubt all outward adornments and show would be cast off as filthy rags and left behind, for all visible things are only temporal and perishable and must be left behind. "Seeing then that all these things shall be dissolved" (burned with fire), in the great day of the Lord, "what manner of persons ought ye to be in all holy conversation and godliness? looking for and hastening unto the coming of the day of God."[20] "Wherefore, beloved, seeing that ye look for such things, be diligent that ye may be found of him in peace, without spot and blameless," 2 Pet. 3. Here then also a girding of the loins should take place. Our Savior says, "Let your loins be girded about, and your lights burning, and ye yourselves like unto men that wait for their Lord."[21]

Stand therefore having your loins girt about with truth "for the day of the Lord will come as a thief in the night, in the which the heavens shall pass away with a great noise, and the elements shall melt with fervent heat; the earth also and the works that are therein shall be burned up."[22] In that great day which "shall burn as an oven, when all the proud and all that do wickedly, shall be as stubble."[23] Then it shall be done with the proud as the Lord threatened to do with the proud king of Babylon, through the prophet Jeremiah, "Behold I am against thee, O thou most proud, saith the

---

19   Ephesians 4:24.
20   2 Peter 3:11-12a.
21   Luke 12:35-36a.
22   2 Peter 3:10.
23   Malachi 4:1a.

Lord God of hosts; for thy day is come, the time that I will visit thee. And the most proud shall stumble and fall, and none shall raise him up, and I will kindle a fire in his cities and it shall devour all round about him," Jer. 50:31, 32. Then indeed shall the proud exclaim, as Solomon says, "What has pride profited us? or what good hath riches with our vaunting brought us? All those things are passed away like a shadow, and as a post that hasteth by," Wisdom 5:8, 9.

Oh! deceiving and uncertain riches! How many thousands and millions of the human race have been so miserably deceived thereby, led into pride and arrogance, and brought to ruin and destruction? How many parents labor day and night to gather riches for their children, who again waste the hard-earned treasures in pride and extravagance? With this same gathered wealth the parents often furnish Satan with gins and nets with which he drags their children into hell. "For those that will be rich," says the apostle, "fall into temptation and a snare, and into many foolish and hurtful lusts, which drown men in destruction and perdition."[24]

But how will it be with those who are already rich? "How hardly shall they that have riches enter into the kingdom of God,"[25] says the Savior. It is mostly the case when a man becomes rich in temporal goods, he becomes proud and lifted up in himself, and the outward adornment and display ever increaseth until frequently, he finally leaves and forgets God his Creator. Too often we see that as temporal riches increase with a man, he decreases and grows poorer in spiritual and heavenly treasures; and yet perhaps he says to himself, "I am rich and increased with goods, and have need of nothing,"[26] and knoweth not (with all his imaginary wealth, both temporal and spiritual), that he is wretched, miserable, poor, blind, and naked. Thus is he also that layeth up treasures for himself and is not rich toward God, Luke 12:21. So secure, blind, proud, and lifted up a man may become by the deception of riches. Therefore, Let sudden fear come upon you, all ye proud women, and maidens, ye men and youth, yea tremble, Oh! ye careless ones, for the day of death is coming and may be

24   1 Timothy 6:9.
25   Mark 10:23.
26   Revelation 3:17.

near at the door. Then with Micah, you will have to exclaim, (when all your gods, such as riches, lust of the flesh, lust of the eye, and the pride of life, will at once be taken from you and destroyed), what have I more?

The day of judgment also is at hand and who knows how near it is? There "we must all appear before the judgment seat of Christ, that every one may receive the things done in his body, according to that he hath done, whether it be good or bad."[27] Terrible will it be for all the proud when they must there appear! Oh! prepare to meet your God!

In Isaiah 33:14 we read, "The sinners in Zion are afraid; fearfulness (trembling, German translation), hath surprised the hypocrites [and they say], Who among us shall dwell with everlasting burnings? He that walketh righteously, and speaketh uprightly." A similar fear and trembling will also overtake all the careless ones, at the coming day of judgment, who would not tremble in the day of grace, as did the jailor at Philippi, who came trembling and fell down before Paul and Silas, "and said, sirs, What must I do to be saved?"[28] The safe and sure way was pointed out to him and he accepted it. Follow his example and you will not need to tremble in the day of judgment. Therefore be not high-minded, but fear, "work out your salvation with fear and trembling, for the great day of his wrath is coming, and who shall be able to stand?"[29]

Though this discourse is directed chiefly to the proud women and maidens, the proud men and youths must not by any means feel themselves excluded from its teachings, admonitions, instructions, and warnings, for to them, too, these words are directed. May the merciful Father bestow his blessing upon them, that they may indeed be such a voice of alarm, that through them many proud and careless souls may be awakened and brought to Jesus, the humble Lamb, to the honor and glory of God. Amen.

---

27   2 Corinthians 5:10.
28   Acts 16:30.
29   Revelation 6:17.

O! be terrified, you proud women,[30]
And tremble, you self-confident.
For a great horror will yet descend over the godless.
O! think upon the future,
Prepare yourselves for the Judgment;
Think how blessed the godly will be
When the Great Day will arrive.

Also you proud maidens, listen,
Tremble and be terrified.
Be converted to Jesus
Since He continues to call you.
Purify yourselves from pomp in clothing
Even though the world already laughs at you.
Bow yourselves right before Jesus
So will He magnificently adorn you.

Also all you proud men
Repent, and seek Light
Think upon the trumpet sound
That will awake everyone to Judgment.
All of you are aware
that a great day is at hand.
Yes a day, 'tis very serious,
Which certainly will still finally come.

---

30   In the original, this was a German poem. It is here translated by Aaron Burkholder; reviewed by Leonard Gross.

Also you proud youth, take heed,
Tremble before the Judge's bench.
Also listen to what the Word is still teaching:
There is a lake of fire
Prepared for the devil.
And also for haughty people,
Where all will be sent
Who here do not heed the warning.

Now let all the proud people together
Give account,
Otherwise you must be eternally damned.
Don't risk it any longer
Affluence, pride, honor, and money
Do not help you at the end of the world.
You must be born again,
If you want to escape the anguish of hell.

Thoughts on the Same Subject by Other Authors.

"The use of jewelry and gay and costly attire may be attributed to three causes. 1st. A natural taste for them. 2nd. A desire to gratify others. 3rd. The supposed necessity of compliance with the imperious dictates of fashion.

"IT IS A FACT that in *all* Evangelical churches there are more or fewer, who are taught by the Spirit, to refrain from such gratifications (the wearing of jewelry and gay and costly attire), and we submit that as a general rule, in all churches the most holy and useful persons, systematically and conscientiously, stand aloof from all such practices."—*Christ and Adornments.*[1]

"A MARTYR TO FASHION would be the most truthful, if not the most appropriate epitaph that could be written upon the tombstones" of thousands who die in our land. "In many a professedly Christian home, the first lesson a child learns is how to dress in the prevailing style."—*Woman's Work for Jesus.*[2]

"A FEW YEARS AGO, a young woman was living in one of our large cities who was the child of wealthy parents. She was fond of the gay pleasures of the city, moved in the highest circles of fashion and lived as though there was no higher world. While thus living in pleasure and the enjoyments of all worldly vanities, she, upon a certain occasion, attended public worship, where the Spirit of God awakened in her the consciousness of sin, and she was bowed down in great anguish, at the thought of her guilt. Her heaviness of heart was soon discovered by her family at home, and her parents were in consternation lest their beautiful daughter should leave the giddy circles of pleasure, for the service of God. They besought her and commanded her to return to the gay follies of the vain and deceitful world. But an inward power wrought upon her heart so that she was greatly troubled in her mind. Fi-

---

1   S. H. Platt, *Christ and Adornments*, 1867, Western Tract and Book Society, pp. 8, 45-46.
2   Annie Wittenmyer, *Women's Work for Jesus*, 1871, published by author, p. 123.

nally her parents made another effort to win her back to the gay society they loved, by promising to give her the richest dress that could be purchased in the city of New York, if she would attend a certain pleasure party. The fatal bribe succeeded. With much reluctance she consented, went to enjoy the gay festivities of the occasion, and immediately lost all religious emotions. Her convictions had fled, and she felt no longer any regard for the things of God. The desire of the parents was accomplished, but the season of their pleasure was short. Disease overtook the young woman and in another week she lay at the point of death. The physician could do nothing; she was past human help. When she was told that there was no hope, that she must die, she lay for a few moments in perfect silence, as if surveying the past and looking into the future. Then arousing herself she told the servant to bring her that dress and hang it upon the post of the bed. Then, calling her parents, who in a few minutes stood weeping around her bedside. She looked upon each of them for a time, then lifting her hand, and pointing to the dress, she said with the terrible calmness of despair, *'Father, mother, there is the price of my soul.'*[3] What a terrible comment on the love of pleasure and the consequence of pride and display.

IT IS ARGUED: 'It does not matter what the outward adornings are, if only the heart is right.'

"True; but if the heart is right, and is kept in a proper frame, *everything else will be set right.*"

"THE OUTWARD LIFE is the index to the heart."

"AS THE HANDS upon the dial plate indicate the hours of the day, so the outward adornings and words reveal the advance of the soul in spiritual life."—*Christ and Adornments.*[4]

---

3   S. H. Platt, *Christ and Adornments*, 1867, Western Tract and Book Society, pp. 102-104. (Brenneman's quotation is not exact.)
4   Actually from Annie Wittenmyer, *Women's Work for Jesus*, 1871, published by author, p. 127.

"Ye Cannot Serve God and Mammon." By H. B. Brenneman.[1]

Oh, why are the sons and the daughters
    Of Adam so vain and so gay?
And why are they growing more haughty,
    More worldly and proud every day?

But why need we ask or e'en wonder,
    Why fashion and folly do reign,
With those who are seeking the honor
    Of this world's extended domain?

Old Satan, that dreadful deceiver
    The father of folly and sin,
Is leading them on at his pleasure,
    Because he is reigning within.

E'en some who profess to be Christians,
    And talk of religion within;
Still show by their outward adorning
    With Jesus they never have been.

They say that it makes little diff'rence—
    That clothes which look gaily and bright
May be worn by the best of the Christians,
    "If only the heart is all right."

The apostle declares in plain language,
    As plain as with words can be told,
If any are void of Christ's Spirit, [Rom. 8:9]
    They do not belong to his fold.

---

1   Henry Brenneman was John M. Brenneman's brother.

He speaks too of outward adorning,
    Of plaiting the hair—and he told,
Of putting on costly apparel, [1 Tim. 2:9]
    And wearing of pearls and of gold.

"In like manner also that women
    In modest apparel be adorned,"
For thus it is right and becoming, [1 Tim. 2:10]
    And not to this world be conformed.

All those who are led by the Spirit,
    Abhor what is idle and vain;
They have *no desire* to wear it,
    And bring their dear Savior to shame.

Now those who profess to be Christians,
    And still love what Christ has condemned,
Are not yet possessed of his Spirit,
    And are not yet what they pretend.

Some too, who profess to be fighting
    For Christ and his glorious cause,
But go forth their enemies smiting,
    Contrary to Christ and his laws.

Some who with their God made a cov'nant,
    And vowed that to him they would cleave,
To walk in his ways and commandments,
    And never their Savior would leave.

But soon they forget what they've promised;
    Take part with the worldly and vain—
Like the sow that is washed in clean water,
    Returns to the mire again.

O, be not deceived, men and women,
    Turn from that which evil appears—
"Ye cannot serve God and serve mammon,"
    For thus Christ, the Savior declares.

The Coming of Christ
By J. M. Brenneman

Behold I come quickly: and my reward is with me, Rev. 22:12.

Behold the Lord will quickly come,
    The time is surely close at hand,
When he shall call his ransomed home
    To Canaan's peaceful, happy land.

Behold he bringeth a reward
    For all who serve him faithful here;
Rejoice, ye saints, go meet your Lord,
    And shed no more a mournful tear.

Behold, he cometh with the clouds,
    All eyes shall see him, Lord of all;
With them who pierced him, causing wounds,
    All kindreds wailing prostrate fall.

Behold the Heavens with great noise
    Now pass away, and earth shall burn;
The trumpet sounds with thunder voice,
    While sleeping millions now return.

Behold him on his throne so high,
    In splendid glorious majesty:
All nations to him drawing nigh,
    To hear their final destiny.

Behold the judge of quick and dead,
    Thus fixed upon his glorious throne;
Who once his precious blood did shed—
    The bitter winepress trod alone.

Behold the man who once was crowned
  With prickly thorns by wicked hands;
With glory crowned he'll now confound
  All those who spurned at his commands.

Behold He now will separate,
  As doth a shepherd, goats from sheep;
Each now to his eternal state
  Be placed, his due reward to reap.

His sheep he'll set to his right hand
  And say, Come, ye my Father's blest,
The kingdom, in that happy land
  Prepared, inherit: come to rest.

But those who on his left are found,
  Must hear the awful sentence passed;
"Depart ye cursed," (oh, dreadful sound!)
  Into the fire they will be cast.

Which for the devil was prepared,
  And for his angels long ago;
So Jesus has himself declared,
  Oh, what an awful place of woe!

Take warning now, ye sinners all,
  For safety flee to mercy's gate;
In Jesus' Name for mercy call,
  Oh, pray and cry before too late!

Also by John M. Brenneman

Christianity and War

In a nation torn in two by the strife of the Civil War, some dared to question whether Christians could participate in the killing. In 1863, soon after the Battle of Gettysburg, John M. Brenneman wrote to explain Anabaptist convictions against participation in warfare. He began by explaining that a true Christian is one who follows Christ's example, who is obedient to Christ, and who is filled with the Spirit of Christ. Having established this definition, he uses it to show that war is completely inconsistent with a Christian profession. The life of peace, love, and nonresistance is the life of obedience and following Jesus, and the only way of living which is truly spiritual.

Encouragement to Penitent Sinners

Nothing can be more needful, and nothing should interest a sinner more deeply, than a true conversion to God. Upon this depends his eternal well-being! A sinner under conviction should have a correct and clear understanding of true conversion so that he be not led astray by the deception of a false conversion.

This books aims to reveal true Gospel conversion in as plain and comprehensive manner as is possible, so that no convicted sinner will, after reading it, have reason to complain that the subject is too dark, mysterious, and unintelligible.

For more excellent titles and other material by the same
author, call or write for a free catalog:

Sermon on the Mount Publishing

P.O. Box 246
Manchester, MI 48158
(734) 428-0488

the-witness@sbcglobal.net

www.kingdomreading.com

Printed in Great Britain
by Amazon